MY
ADDRESS BOOK:
A WAY OF REMEMBERING

SUSAN WOODALL

ISBN: 1469913127
ISBN 13: 9781469913124

Library of Congress Control Number: 2012901234
CreateSpace, North Charleston, SC

For Sunny and Serena

TABLE OF CONTENTS

INTRODUCTION VII

CHAPTER ONE
9 Brady Avenue, New Britain, Connecticut.................... 3

CHAPTER TWO
9 Laurel Road, New Britain, Connecticut ....,............... 7

CHAPTER THREE
Beech Tree Lane, West Hartford, Connecticut 13

CHAPTER FOUR
60 East 12th Street, New York, New York.....................19

CHAPTER FIVE
230 East 15th Street, New York, New York 23

CHAPTER SIX
222 Martling Avenue, Tarrytown, New York.................27

CHAPTER SEVEN
6 Leawood Drive, Briarcliff Manor, New York 31

CHAPTER EIGHT
20 Overton Road, Ossining, New York.....................35

CHAPTER NINE

35 South State Road, Briarcliff Manor, New York............39

CHAPTER TEN

336 Cherry Street, Bedford Hills, New York 43

CHAPTER ELEVEN

10 Upland Road North, Bedford, New York.................47

CHAPTER TWELVE

313 Leslie Avenue, West Lafayette, Indiana 57

CHAPTER THIRTEEN

4039 Moss Creek, West Lafayette, Indiana...................63

CHAPTER FOURTEEN

330 West Diversey Parkway, Chicago, Illinois ....:.69

CHAPTER FIFTEEN

64 Rimmon Road, Woodbridge, Connecticut 73

CHAPTER SIXTEEN

40 Temple Court, New Haven, Connecticut 81

CHAPTER SEVENTEEN

375 Race Hill Road, Madison, Connecticut 87

INDEX TO NAMES **94**

INTRODUCTION

Houses have always played an important part in my life. Not only the houses themselves, but their addresses. When I was a little girl, my mother, who was an interior decorator, often used to take me driving around town looking at neighborhoods. She taught me the concept that where a person lived revealed a lot about him or her. Not only the neighborhood, but the house. People could dress beautifully and drive fancy cars, but if the house or the neighborhood didn't match up to that level, that would often mean they were phony, or just trying to impress others. Conversely, some people wore modest clothes, drove ordinary cars, and yet lived in fancy neighborhoods, or in stately homes. That meant they probably had old money and didn't need to impress others. Then there were people who lived in fancy, often garish houses, and may or may not have driven similar cars. These people, my mother deemed "nouveau riche." In her eyes, that was the worst label a person could have. And so, at a very young age, I became very conscious of the social significance of "address."

As an adult, I spent almost seventeen years as a real estate broker. That career was a conflicted one for me. I was always fascinated by that old relationship of people to their houses, and also by how a home's interior reveals so much about its occupants. The stress-filled business of buying and selling houses for clients and customers fascinated me much less, and I eventually retired. But

I have, at least until recently, looked upon real estate as a worthy investment.

This journal is a tribute to and a fond remembrance of the houses in my life. It was prompted by a significant move in 1993, from New York to Indiana. Until that time, I had lived within a radius of 125 miles: from Hartford, Connecticut to New York City. Within that radius, I had moved many times; 10, not including college, to be exact. But in 1993, my husband made a long-awaited career change from industry to university and we found ourselves in a place we had never been before. I wanted to document those places that I had lived in, and continue to live in. All our families had lived in and been brought up on the East Coast. Now we were moving to the Heartland. It was an amazing journey, and it continues still.

I must add that I have since returned to my home state of Connecticut and it's quite different from what I had remembered. For one thing, when I left Connecticut in 1964, there was no state income tax. Now there is.

The cities of Hartford and West Hartford are vastly different from when I was a child. While Hartford has declined, West Hartford has thrived.

But there is a mild sadness I was surprised to experience in returning "home." My children, now adults with their own lives, no longer live in the vicinity. My older daughter Sunny lives in Chicago, and my younger daughter Serena lives in Miami Beach. My sister is the only family I have left here in Connecticut, but due to the vagaries of our lives, we see each other rarely. And so, this journey of mine has been a mixed blessing. Nevertheless, I am very happy to have returned to the place of my birth and childhood.

This journal is also a plea for roots. For settling down. The older I get, the more I realize that settling down can be advantageous to one's emotional, financial, and spiritual well-being.

This history of the houses and addresses I've had is a way of saying who I am. Not completely, of course. But it does tell a lot, I think.

9 BRADY AVENUE
NEW BRITAIN, CONNECTICUT 06052

CHAPTER ONE

This is the house I lived in when I was born. I have few recollections of it, except through photographs. According to notes left to me by my father, he and my mother bought this house in 1941, three years before my birth, for $8,000, with a 4 percent mortgage, unamortized. The mortgage payments amounted to $300 per year!

Dad did extensive renovations on this house, helped by friends and neighbors, including building a recreation room with pecky cypress paneling, and hand-painted murals by his friend Emil Brandt, a Holocaust refugee.

Brady Avenue was a street where my parents had many friends. I remember their friends stopping by for informal visits, especially on Sunday afternoons, and my parents and I doing the same by visiting friends and neighbors, just popping by.

One friend in particular, Molly Raphael, who lived down the street with her husband, Buddy, was a character. Molly today would be considered a "hippie," or at least an artistic type. She had long hair with a bandana wrapped around it, and she herself was long and lanky. I can picture her even now, relaxing on her porch with a cigarette in one hand and a glass of iced coffee in the other.

I was three years old when we moved away from it. There is a picture of me, around the age of three, in my bedroom, with my bathrobe and nightie on. My hair is piled high up on my head. I'm holding my Teddy bear, which I remember very well. The picture is in black and white, but I visualize the wallpaper in the bedroom as being pink and white stripes with big pink flowers cascading down the stripes. It would be similar to Laura Ashley today, but in the forties mode.

The house was on a good-sized piece of property for New Britain in those days, at least by my father's standards. The yard, according to his notes, was 70 feet by 100 feet. Dad was a diligent gardener. He loved tending to vegetables, especially his favorite tomatoes, and cultivating lovely flowers as well. Mother, ever the city girl, preferred concentrating her energies into beautifying the interior of the house.

When they moved to Brady Avenue, Mother decided to go Victorian.

There was a round mahogany pedestal table with clawed feet for the dining room. A mahogany chest with a marble top and intricate grape leaves for pull handles held Mother's silver, table linens and extra serving pieces. A large matching mirror accompanied the chest. There was a smaller mate to that "grape chest" as we called it, which belonged to my mother's aunt, Lee. Mother made sure, once Aunt Lee died, that she, Mother, secured that smaller chest.

The living room was furnished with a Victorian couch, tufted in grey velvet, and two tufted easy chairs, as well as a small baby grand piano.

Going back to this house in 1992, to take the photograph, it seemed like a real Andy Hardy type of neighborhood. Houses close together, sidewalks, family neighborhood. Now there's a basketball hoop in the front driveway. As with so many of the houses we've revisited, vinyl siding has replaced clapboard or shingle. A slice of Middle America, a/k/a New Britain! Ironically, this house comes close to the one we moved to in West Lafayette, Indiana. Even to the blue vinyl siding.

When it was time to move, Dad recalled that he and Mother swapped houses with Emory Corbin, the owner of 9 Laurel Road. Emory was from the esteemed Corbin Family of New Britain, but apparently, Emory fell on hard times, due to his alcoholism, and hence, the switcheroo. In Dad's inimitable words:

"The Corbins moved into a clean, well-maintained place. We moved into a disaster."

———◆———

9 LAUREL ROAD
NEW BRITAIN, CONNECTICUT 06052

CHAPTER TWO

This 3-storied Tudor-styled house I remember very well. This was the house of my childhood. Emory Corbin swapped it for the Brady Avenue house with my parents. Emory Corbin came from the family of Corbin Locks, a pre-eminent manufacturing company in the city of New Britain, Connecticut, which billed itself as "The Hardware Capital of the World."

Because of the deplorable condition of the house (Dad told me they found empty liquor bottles stashed in closets, cupboards and other obscure places for years afterwards), my parents spent $10,000 remodeling it, including a new roof, a new heating system, carpeting, painting, and the like.

One interesting bonus of the house, since it belonged to a scion of a hardware factory, was that all the hardware in the house was silver-plated, and all locks were keyed to a master lock, which my father had keyed additionally to his business locks.

The landscaping was spectacular, with a specimen iris bed, huge peonies bordering the sloping curved driveway, and prized tulip bulbs in the formal gardens.

It was on a lovely street which we called the circle. Today, it would be called a cul-de-sac. In the middle of the circle was a round of grass (I don't know who mowed it) with a big evergreen tree in the middle. At Christmastime, this tree was decorated with lights. There were about seven houses on this end of the street, mostly all Tudors. They were all quite substantial, considering New Britain was a working-class, factory town. Our next door neighbors were the Ways to the left and the Duncans to the right. I was especially fond of Katie and Stan Duncan. They had two children, Teddy and Tootie, who were much older than I was. It was the Korean War and Teddy was in the Navy. Katie had a big map of the world up on the wall of her breakfast nook, with yarn delineating the route of Teddy's ship in the Pacific. That was one way I learned geography!

The Duncans played croquet on a special court they had built in their backyard. Rising above the court on a gentle slope was a flagstone patio with lawn furniture. The Duncans and their friends would sit there and drink beer and smoke cigarettes while they played. I always thought they had the best fun! It was all so casual and relaxed. I remember Katie calling her sofa in the living room a "davenport." I still don't know where that term comes from.

Back to Number 9, our house. It seemed like such a big house at the time. Upon revisiting it forty years later, it shrank somewhat.

The lay-out included an entrance foyer, with a stairway up ahead, and a center hall leading back and around to the kitchen; a powder room, a den and a porch. The living room was off to one side of the center hall, with a wood-paneled den off of that. The living room had a fireplace and windows that faced the porch. Mother had the living room furnished in Victorian style, with soft grey velvet upholstered chairs and sofa and carpet. Green and violet fabric complemented the grey. It seemed so lush and elegant to me. The den had knotty pine cabinets and bookcases that my father built. He was very handy. The TV, when we finally got one, was in there.

The dining room was on the opposite side of the center hall. The walls were papered in grey, green and purple, with a grape motif. The furniture was still Victorian and quite formal. Adjacent to the dining room was a butler's pantry, with glass fronted cupboards containing dishes and glassware. I can recall green marbleized linoleum on the floor of the pantry and the kitchen. The dining room floor was carpeted like the living room.

The kitchen was papered in white with green ivy. Even the insides of the cabinets were papered. We didn't have a dishwasher for quite a while. One of my chores was to dry the dishes after dinner. I couldn't wait until we got a dishwasher, so I wouldn't have to dry dishes anymore!

I had two bedrooms in that house; a winter and a summer bedroom. The winter bedroom was up in the front of the house, across from my parents' room. It was papered in a pink cabbage rose pattern. My furniture was painted white, with a touch of gold and pink. Sort of French and very feminine. My summer bedroom was at the back of the house, across the hall from where my baby sister's room would be. But she wouldn't be arriving on the scene for a few years yet. This room was done originally in green. After Kathe was born, in 1951, my bedroom was redone. Dad had built me a doll's cabinet to house my growing collection of show dolls. The walls were papered with a small print of aqua background and little brown leaves. Very colonial. My furniture there was colonial knotty pine. My grandmother bought me a desk to go with my bureau. I kept that furniture all through the years until recently.

My sister's bedroom had a red spotted linoleum floor. The walls were white. It was a small room, but cheerful. It looked out onto the backyard. The hall bath there was tiled in Easter egg purple and yellow. The front hall bath, the master, was tiled in green. Then there was a third floor, which contained Mother's sewing room and an attic.

The room I remember most vividly was Mother and Dad's bedroom. The carpet was off-white; the walls were papered in a red and ivory toile print and the draperies, bed cover and dressing table were swathed in matching fabric. Over Mother's dressing table, which Dad had built into the wall, was a wall mirror, with crystal sconces on either side. Very formal and elegant. I used to love to play dress-up with Mother's jewelry and clothing at that dressing table. And when I was sick, I would stay in their bed. They put me back in my own bed at night.

It seemed like we must have been quite rich to have a house like that. But in truth, we weren't. Dad was able to charge a lot of our expenses to his business, the Latimer Laundry, so we had the lovely gardens tended by his employees, as well as the services of a maid. Mother had a little buzzer under the dining table and whenever she needed to call the maid, Lily Engblom, she would buzz her.

My birthday parties were held in that dining room. Most kids' parties were held in their recreation rooms; mine were in our formal dining room. My birthday was right near Halloween so the motif was orange and black and pumpkins and such. We have pictures of all us kids sitting around the dining table having cake and ice cream. Mother had silver candelabra with black candles in them. I loved that house, but I do remember crying to Mother, "Why can't we have a new house?" Soon enough we did.

My parents sold this house in 1954 for $35,000, which was the largest price for a single-family home in New Britain at that time. And even though we moved from a 5 bedroom house to a 3 bedroom house, it was still a move up in real estate value, because of location.

Beech Tree Lane
West Hartford, Connecticut 06107

CHAPTER THREE

This was a new house. The builder was a man named Bill Bishop. I remember the discussions about him from my parents. He was an individualist and it showed in his house. The house was very well-built, but a little unusual; for example, the living rooms walls were painted a deep purple. Not exactly what you'd expect for a house built for speculation. The kitchen walls were painted a deep teal. This turned out to be a blessing in disguise, for the house didn't sell as quickly as the builder would have liked and my parents were able to get a "good deal." They purchased it unfinished for $35,000. The walls were soon painted off-white.

There were a couple of things I'd like to note in remembrance of this house. First of all, it was in West Hartford. We made the move in 1954, from New Britain to West Hartford, according to Mother, because the schools were better there. I was entering the sixth grade and I certainly noticed a big difference. West Hartford was just a better place to live. It was relatively affluent, compared with the working-class atmosphere of New Britain.

The second thing regarding this house was that it was the smallest house in the neighborhood. It was still a very nice house, but the others on the street, a small private road off the prestigious

Hunter Drive, were far more impressive. This is an excellent situation to be in, real-estate-wise. But a few of our neighbors made us feel a little like the poor relations on the block. We were definitely not welcomed with open arms. Nevertheless, we were soon on friendly terms with most of them, except for the Weinsteins, our neighbors directly to the left of us. Mrs. Weinstein especially, had a neighborhood reputation as being the bitch on the block. She even had a mean and nasty old dog.

To our right, just up a small hill, were the Stahls. They were an older couple who had custom built their home and it was beautiful. The rest of the neighbors included the Myers, the Rosenthals, the Giddons, the Kaplans, and the Chesters. The whole larger neighborhood, which included Hunter Drive and the Westborough Woods, was very Wasp. Beech Tree Lane was a little Jewish enclave.

One thing I loved about the house was that many of the interior walls were paneled in solid wood, tongue-in-groove, not four-by-eight sheets. This was an indication of quality; it was also very attractive and very practical. The living room was paneled in bleached white oak. It had a huge picture window overlooking the back yard and once the remaining plastered wall was changed from its original dark purple to off-white, the whole room, all thirty feet of it, was light and open.

Mother carpeted the floor with an oatmeal wool loop broadloom. It was calming and inviting. One of the short walls had built-in bookcases and a desk. The wall opposite the picture window had a brick fireplace, which Mother had painted off-white, and a raised hearth of flagstone, which made for nice additional seating right by the fireplace.

My bedroom, which had originally been planned as a den (and as soon as I was married, nine years later, was returned to that state), was paneled in a warm cherry wood. It too, had built-in bookcases on one wall, and an unusual louvered picture window facing the backyard. It was a small but cozy room. About a week after we moved, during the summer of 1954, when I was ten, I got an attack of appendicitis and had to be rushed to Hartford Hospital for an appendectomy. I was in the hospital for about a week, and when I returned home, my room had been papered and decorated in aqua and brown, the same paper that had been my room at Laurel Road in New Britain. Was I surprised! My only regret was that I was not consulted at all about it. I had no choice.

The basement, which was unfinished when we bought the house, was very large, as ranch basements often are. Dad finished off a part of it into a pine-paneled recreation room. It too had a fireplace (there was a brick fireplace and hearth in the kitchen as well) and Dad built bookcases and installed a TV into the wall. He tiled the floor in a spotted asphalt checkerboard pattern of beige and black squares.

The big negative about the house was that it was quite small, and most especially that my bedroom was right off the living room and I had very little privacy. My room was the first one in the bed-room hallway, and I had to cross the hall to get to the bathroom. I could hear everything going on in the living room when I was in my bedroom, and looking back now, I guess anyone who was in the living room could hear anything that was going on in my bedroom.

Many a tear fell in that bedroom.

One dating episode that I remember with great horror was being invited to the Junior Prom of our competing high school,

Hall High. I barely knew the young man who invited me, as we had just recently met at some Jewish youth group activity. But he was an attractive and very popular guy and I accepted his invitation. When I asked my parents for permission to go to his prom, they naturally inquired about who was this young man? I told them his name and the investigation proceeded.

His name was Mike, and to my parent's chagrin, he lived in a poor neighborhood. They were not pleased. They didn't know his parents, and they were very wary of my going out with a person of an obvious "lower class." (This search for where a person lived was often the determining factor in my parent's appraisal of character definition, unfortunately.)

They gave their very reluctant permission for me to attend the prom with Mike, but with the almost impossible rule of a curfew of ten o'clock.

"Mother!" I cried, "Ten o'clock for a Junior Prom? That's absurd! No one goes home from the prom that early. There will be parties afterwards, starting at midnight! Please, let me stay out 'til at least mid-night!"

My parents were adamant. They didn't know this boy and they felt he came from "the wrong side of the tracks." They would not budge. I was determined to go and enjoy the prom with Mike and fudge a bit on the curfew. I told him I had to be home by eleven, but maybe we could be a few minutes late.

It turned out, Mike was chosen to be "King of the Prom," and of course, there were celebrations all around. I was torn by knowing that I was defying my parents, but still compromising my date and myself. It was a no-win situation.

I got home around midnight to a pair of furious and growling parents, and an incredulous and unhappy date. I never heard from Mike again but I certainly understood why. It was so embarrassing!

I did, however, continue to date various young men more to my parents' approval, culminating with meeting Steve Golding in my freshman year of college.

Beech Tree Lane was the house from which I was married. That was the house where my children first came to visit their Grandma and Grandpa. That was the first house I remember best. When my parents sold that house, in 1974, to move into a condominium in near-by Farmington, I no longer had a childhood home. I never felt any proprietary interest in the condo. Nor should I have. I felt more like a guest instead of a family member in my parents' home from now on.

60 East 12th Street
New York, New York 10003

CHAPTER FOUR

This white brick apartment building was completed in 1964, right before my marriage to Stephen L. Golding, which took place on August 2 of that year. Steve, living at 33 Washington Square West, Haydon Hall, at the New York University Law School, where he was a first year student, had scouted out the building in advance.

A friend of Steve's from their Brown University days, Stu Hauser, was getting married that same summer, and he was living across the street from 60 East 12th at 77 East 12th Street. These were the only two apartments we saw and we preferred 60 East 12th. This impulsive choosing of places to live was to become a pattern throughout my life.

We moved our possessions into the brand-new space before our wedding and when we returned from our honeymoon in Bermuda, a week afterwards, we entered our apartment and our new life together. It was no more than a ten-minute walk to Washington Square, where I would complete my bachelor's degree at New York University, and Steve would complete his law degree (1966) and later his Master's of Law in Taxation one year after that, in 1967.

Our apartment was in the middle of the building and right in front of the elevator, on the top floor. I had never lived in an apartment house before, nor in New York City, and I learned something right off the bat: there are no floors numbered 13 in apartment houses in New York City! So our apartment was ostensibly on the 14th floor. But who's counting?

The apartment was called a "junior one bedroom" or "junior three". It had a sleeping alcove off the living room with the bathroom off that. Our landlord offered to put up a partition for us so that we would have a private bedroom. There were louvered doors separating the bedroom from the living room. The kitchen was an efficiency, with a dining area off that. We thought it was terrific at the time, all fresh and new – and ours. I couldn't wait to decorate it. We bought a remnant of blue carpet (white walls, of course), had a blue print sofa and accented it with burnt orange throw pillows. We thought it was very chic. For this apartment we paid $160 a month in rent.

Now that I was a married lady, even though we were both still in school, my attitude towards my studies was that I was going to work. I was surprised to find that I actually liked NYU and found the courses more stimulating than some I had taken at Connecticut College for Women in New London, from where I had transferred.

Our neighborhood was exciting and convenient. The Strand Book Store, a landmark for used books, was right across the street, on the corner of Broadway and 12th. We could get the uptown bus on the other corner, at 4th Avenue to go to visit my grandmother, which we did quite frequently. She lived at 55 East 87th Street.

On the way home from school was a very nice Gristede's supermarket where I shopped. We stayed in that apartment until 1967, until Steve finished his tax graduate program.

A memorable event occurred while we were living on 12th Street: the big blackout of 1965. I was in class at NYU, late in the afternoon. We were released from class and we walked down many flights of stairs from our classroom to the street, as the elevators were no longer working. As I trudged up University Place towards 12th Street, I asked a police officer who was directing traffic if the power outage went up as far as 14th Street. He looked at me incredulously and said,

"Lady, all of New York is out!"

It turned out most of the Northeast was out! I walked up the thirteen flights of stairs to our apartment. By that time, it was dark. The apartment house was lit with candles and there was a party atmosphere throughout. Steve came home soon thereafter and we and our neighbors got together for a pot luck dinner. We were not surprised to learn that the birth rate nine months later had skyrocketed!

230 East 15th Street
New York, New York 10003

Chapter Five

We made the big move in 1967 to this apartment. It was only three blocks away, so convenient that we were able to bring most of our things over from 12th Street by shopping cart! The heavy furniture we allowed The Seven Santini Brothers to move for us. This was a much nicer apartment, as well it should have been. The rent was $235 a month.

At first, Steve wondered how we would be able to afford it, but soon enough, that was not a problem. Steve's poker games, as well as the Go-Go years of the stock market, made the rent very affordable.

We were on the sixth floor, at the end of the hall, in a spacious full one-bedroom. It was called a floor-through apartment because it spanned the entire width of the building. Our bedroom had windows facing the back (towards 14th Street), and our living room had windows overlooking our patio and out onto 15th Street and Stuyvesant Square, very quaint and enclosed by black wrought iron gates. One could say "Gramercy Park South" and some landlords did. The lobby of this building was much more lavish than 12th Street. We were coming up in the world. We were now part of the newly labeled "Saturday Generation," so-called by Bloomingdale's.

There was a spacious entry foyer with parquet floors. The kitchen was directly ahead; the living room was to the right; the bedroom and bath were to the left. Now that I had graduated and was an employed teacher (making $5,400 a year), we were able to afford some decent furniture. We changed the décor slightly from our previous white walls with blue carpet and orange accents. In this apartment, while we still had white walls, we moved the blue rug into our bedroom, and installed yellow wall-to-wall carpet in the living room. We purchased the carpet and most of the furniture from Sloane's on Fifth Avenue, which was a prestigious furniture store in its day.

That turned out to be a good thing. Our living room faced 15th Street, on the 6th floor, with a terrace overlooking Stuyvesant Park. We often used the terrace but what we didn't realize until after the fact was that there was a lot of soot in New York City. Keeping the door to the terrace open let in more soot than usual, and soon, our beautiful yellow carpet was grey and sooty. I was devastated. What to do?

I contacted Sloane's and they came to the apartment to inspect. At first they decided to shampoo the carpet. Within 6 months, however, the yellow carpet returned to its dismal grey color, even though we kept the terrace door open to an absolute minimum. Sloane's was contacted again, and to its credit, they declared the yellow carpet defective and replaced it. We never had a problem with the carpet again, but I came to view apartments with terraces in congested cities as less than desirable.

Steve decided to take one more year at law school, post-graduate in taxation. The war in Vietnam was going on and he needed the deferment. He also was undecided as to the practice of law, so this was a way of procrastinating. He was doing very well financially, anyway, in the stock market and with his card games.

I became pregnant in this apartment, and when I was in my seventh month, we decided to move. We needed a bigger place. We moved out in July, 1969, to the suburbs of Westchester County, with high hopes.

———◆———

222 MARTLING AVENUE
TARRYTOWN, NEW YORK 10591

CHAPTER SIX

We found this apartment, called Castle Heights, in The New York Times, just like the ad says!

It was a sub-let. Steve decided he wanted to live in Tarrytown, as his poker game began there. It was a half-hour commute on the Hudson Line of the railroad; just enough time to have a good game. If the train were ever delayed, Steve loved it even more: more time to make money.

We took a second floor, two bedroom apartment with a balcony overlooking the parking lot and the front. Compared to our previous apartment, this was so spacious. I can't remember the rent exactly; I think it was in the mid $300's a month. We had two years left on the lease. We bought a new car when we moved: a 1969 navy blue Buick LeSabre convertible, with air-conditioning. I was very visibly pregnant, and soon we were welcomed by lots of the people who lived at Castle Heights. We made many friends there.

We decided to take a short vacation right after we moved in. After all, soon we would be having a baby, and there would be no more time or freedom for such things. We decided to visit our friends, Suzanne and Harold Mellin in Baltimore, and then go to The Tides Inn in Irvington, VA, and stop at Williamsburg as well.

While we were away, at The Tides Inn, Neil Armstrong became the first astronaut to land on the moon. It was an exciting time! We all watched the event on TV in the lodge. I had to go to the bathroom all night long. The next day we left the inn and drove to the Mellins'. We stayed overnight there. Harold was doing his medical military duty at the National Institute of Health. He remarked that he'd never seen a woman as pregnant as I was in such good shape. I did feel terrific. The pregnancy had been off to a rocky start, but now everything seemed to be just fine. I was anxious to get back to our new home and get ready for the baby.

Soon after we returned from our trip to Williamsburg, we were having coffee with two other couples in the apartment house, both of whose wives were expecting babies the same time I was.

We women were comparing notes on the states of our pregnancies, all our firsts. We all felt wonderful, but the two other women were complaining about the babies kicking a lot and keeping them up at night. Suddenly, I realized, I hadn't felt my baby kick in quite some time – not since we returned from our trip. I tapped on my bulging belly, fully expecting a thump in return. I didn't receive one. I tapped again, and again, no response. My heart started racing, and I excused myself and ran to our apartment to consult my pregnancy bible, a book by the esteemed Dr. Guttmacher.

I looked in the index under "Stillbirth." It was August and the baby was due in September. I read that stillbirth was very rare and often unexplainable. I called my obstetrician and he seemed unconcerned. He advised me to come back into the City the next day, Saturday, and get a fetal heartbeat at the hospital.

Steve and I drove in the following morning, me tapping my rock-hard belly frequently, to no avail. I knew in my bones that something was drastically wrong, even though I felt no pain.

CHAPTER SEVEN

This was our first house. Here's how we came to find it. We had been looking at houses on and off for a couple of years. We were hostage to the vagaries of the stock market for the down payment. A few years earlier, because we had done so well in the market, we had quite a bit of cash. But Steve was still in school and had no verifiable income, so we wouldn't qualify for a mortgage. By the early seventies, when he had a decent job, the market started to fall, and so our down payment would be less. Finally, we decided to just bite the bullet and hop on the house-buying train.

At this point, our budget was around $50,000. We had champagne tastes and a beer budget.

It was our 8th anniversary. We were going out to dinner to celebrate. We had chosen a place called Maison LaFitte, in Briarcliff. I decided I wanted to surprise Steve with a pre-paid bottle of champagne with dinner, so a friend and I drove over to the restaurant to pay for it in advance. It was about 8 miles from Castle Heights. I had also been looking with a Realtor at houses in what turned out to be that very neighborhood. Now, on my own, I decided to drive around this family neighborhood near the restaurant. Driving down one of the streets, my friend noticed a For Sale sign on a house. She urged me to stop and take a look. We did. The woman of the house was home and showed us around. The house was too big for us: it had an in-law apartment with it. When I mentioned this to her, she told me there was a similar house two doors down from hers on the market without the in-law suite, and she graciously wrote down the name and number of the owner.

It was a very hot August day when I first went to visit the Rozinsky house. Entering the front door, I was greeted by cool, refreshing air-conditioning. I was impressed. (I wouldn't take a dislike to air-conditioning until a few years later). The second thing that impressed me about the house was the blue wall-to-wall carpeting and the general good taste in décor. Blue was my favorite color. I encouraged Steve to come over and take a look. He liked the fact that we could buy "direct" and avoid a broker's commission, and he loved the central air-conditioning.

Dr. Irwin Rozinsky was a local dentist. He and his family had been in the house for many years. They helped to mollify our distaste for the cookie-cutter style of the house, a split-level in a development. The house had no character or charm. We would have liked that. But it was affordable and sensible. It had the necessary rooms we needed, as well as amenities, and the neighborhood was very well-maintained, as was the house itself. Besides, we reasoned, in a couple of years, we'd be able to do better. We took the plunge.

The house was actually very livable and good for us with our growing family. Each daughter had a bedroom, although they decided to share one bedroom. Steve papered the walls with a cute print called "Wabbits." It was hot pink and green rabbits. We put in green shag carpeting for them and they loved it. Our bedroom we painted lime green. I don't know what got into us; we must have thought that was cool at the time. I guess we were so happy not to have to have white walls anymore. Boy, how times have changed! We left the main living level alone, with the off white walls and the blue carpeting. Thank God we ran out of money.

On the lower level, was a paneled family room where we set up the TV. The girls hung out there and that's where their friends came and played.

The house was on a third of an acre on a cul-de-sac street. It really was a great starter home for us. It just didn't touch our hearts aesthetically. We stayed there longer than we had anticipated, but we made many improvements, including extending the driveway, replacing the picture window in the dining area with sliding glass doors and a deck. We re-roofed and eventually re-painted, inside and out. We planted trees and flowers. We made friends in the neighborhood. We joined a local tennis and swim club. We were there five years, three years longer than we anticipated. In those five years, though, we made enough money to trade up, just like our predecessors had done before us. But this time, I had entered the real estate business myself. Now I would be buying direct in a slightly different way.

In 1972, we paid $46,500 for Leawood Drive. In 1977 we sold it, through my agency, for $64,500 to customers of mine. We didn't mind paying the commission because of what we found to replace it. The next house we bought we literally fell in love with.

———◆———

20 OVERTON ROAD
OSSINING, NEW YORK 10562

CHAPTER EIGHT

I went to preview this house as part of my job as a sales agent. I had been a Realtor since 1975. It was now 1977. We had gotten this listing in our office, along with two other agencies. The house belonged to the Halsey family, whose ancestors were American naval heroes. The Halseys had six children, but there was plenty of room for all of them in this expansive old Victorian specimen. My heart started palpitating the minute I entered the front door.

There was something about this house that said "you're going to buy me." It was scary. The neighborhood was one of Ossining's finest, right across the street from my principal broker, Carolyn Dwyer. She told me the Halseys just wanted to get rid of the house without any hassles. They had a farm in New Hampshire, amongst other properties, and they were moving there soon. The price they were asking was a give-away price: $76,500. That was for a seven-bedroom, five-bathroom, beautifully-restored Victorian house on nine tenths of a magnificently-landscaped acre in a charming neighborhood. It was barely two miles from Leawood Drive.

Upon entering the front door, I immediately noticed the carved oak banister leading up to the second floor. The ceilings were high; the walls were plaster. There was a front parlor with bay windows and lacy curtains; then a library with bookcases and a fireplace. The living room was large and light, with more bay windows. The dining room was baronial, with one wall mirrored in smoked glass. A full bath and large hall closet on the first floor, and then the kitchen. What a kitchen! It embraced the full back of the house, complete with breakfast room. It took four rings on the telephone before you could walk the length of it.

There was a wet bar and a back porch too. Just outside the kitchen was a beautiful old maple tree which covered a lovely flag-stone patio. A three-car garage, a greenhouse, and a large play-house, the size of a two-car garage completed the picture – almost. I shouldn't neglect to describe the bedrooms and the baths on the two upper levels. Each bedroom had its own bath on the second level. We all had our own rooms, Steve's and mine with an adjoin-ing bath. On the third floor were two large and sunny bedrooms and a door which led to a widow's walk around the outside. The basement was large and unfinished, but in excellent shape. In short, the house was a marvel.

The exterior of the house had been aluminum sided. To paint that house would have been prohibitively expensive. There was a lovely brick walk from the front door around to the patio in the back. The entire property was surrounded by a wrought iron fence. The landscaping was lush and full and contained grape arbors, a small orchard, including two sour cherry trees, and various other specimen plantings. The house was as full of charm as the Leawood Drive house was lacking in it. No wonder we both flipped for it.

When I brought Steve over to see it, the moment he walked in the front door he said, "Let's take it!" When I asked him if he didn't want to see the rest of the house before he made up his mind, he replied, sure, he'd look, but he'd already made up his mind. That house fulfilled our fantasies of grandeur. But it was not to last long. And, it ended in tragedy.

In less than a year, Steve was dead and the girls and I moved out of that magnificent house. I sold most of the furniture, and I made an excellent profit on the sale of the house. But even with that tragedy, I can look back on the house at Overton Road with fondness, as well as with tears. For eleven months, we had a house that filled us with pride.

35 SOUTH STATE ROAD
BRIARCLIFF MANOR, NEW YORK 10510

CHAPTER NINE

This is the bittersweet house. The circumstances under which I bought it and we moved there were tragic. Steve had died in a car crash. And yet, I, and apparently all who were to enter this little house, fell in love with it. It was a charming enchanted cottage. It was perfect for the three of us.

There were a few little ironies connected with this house. First of all, I was a real estate agent and part of any good agent's job was to peruse the "For Sale by Owner" ads, FSBOS, they were called. This was a good source of new listings, the agents' stock in trade. I never did this. But for some strange reason, when the sale of Overton Road became apparent, once and only once, I happened to look in the classified ads and saw this one. I called on it, made the appointment to see it and instantly decided to buy it. I offered full price, which the sellers accepted. I told them I was a Realtor but I was buying it for myself. I was so excited and relieved. We would be able to afford it without a mortgage from the proceeds of Overton Road, as well as some of the proceeds of the life insurance I received at Steve's death. Even though the house was very small, and contained only two bedrooms, I thought we could make do. The two children would share a bedroom. That didn't bother me or them at the time.

I always had a feeling that Steve knew what was going on from his vantage point up in heaven.

And so, Widow Golding and her two daughters, ages five and seven, moved from Overton Road in Ossining to South State Road in Briarcliff Manor. Another irony, I had recently sold a house to the Werners, whose daughter, Jessy, was my daughter, Sunny's best friend and would remain so for many years to come. They had lived in our first neighborhood of Leawood Drive earlier. They were now our neighbors two doors down the street. Susan and Keefe Werner and I were friendly and they would be a big help to me now that I was alone.

The house was ideally situated for us. It was within walking distance of the town library, and recreation, not to mention the village itself. The girls loved it. It was also right across the street from a beautiful stone church, and even though we weren't religious, the sight of that beautiful stone structure and the thoughts of God and spirituality were very comforting to me.

Not only did I feel uplifted by the exquisite charm of the house, I curiously felt very independent and free in owning it. It was, after all, the first time I had ever lived alone, without another adult, ever. Of course, my girls were a great source of comfort and joy to me and I felt an aching chasm at the loss of Steve, but I felt an enormous sense of pride and power in owning my own home completely.

I paid $72,000 for it in July of 1978. I remodeled the kitchen, finally having a blue and white one. I gave the girls the larger of the two bedrooms, and I took the smaller one, for which I bought new furniture, installed wall-to-wall carpeting, and added a second closet. The hall carpet was an attractive blue, and the hall had blue print wallpaper. The dining room was quite spacious, and eventually I covered the walls in a provincial fabric of mauve, rose and black. It was quite an undertaking, but it turned out quite well.

It was in this house that I eventually met Jerry Woodall in the winter of 1981. We soon decided to marry and so we Golding girls left this little cottage and moved to Jerry's house in Bedford Hills, about 8 – 10 miles north. I rented South State Road (until I sold it in 1993 for $227,000). The rental income I received help contribute to the new, enlarged family's coffers. We left Briarcliff in July, 1981.

336 CHERRY STREET
BEDFORD HILLS, NEW YORK 10507

CHAPTER TEN

About the time that I was buying the house in Briarcliff, Jerry Woodall and his wife then were buying this house in Bedford Hills. She and her children moved out right before Jerry and I met. When I first came upon the scene, Jerry was living there, sort of, with two of his three children, Marshall, aged 16, and Debi, aged 14. (Chandler, the oldest son, was living on his own.) Jerry was actually commuting to Cornell University in Ithaca, New York, for part of the week to get his PhD, while maintaining his job as a research scientist at IBM in Yorktown Heights, New York. Additionally, he was seeing me and spending as much time with me and my children in Briarcliff as possible.

The Cherry Street house (not to mention his children!) was, needless to say, rather neglected.

When I first laid eyes on the house, I could tell it had once been a charming, even gracious house, but a very long time ago. Now, it looked as though a war had been waged in it, and it had. A divorce war. Solid oak paneled doors had been bashed in. Light bulbs were dangling from their sockets. Bathrooms were lacking the woman's touch, to put it mildly. Floors were scuffed and scummy. It made me sad and even angry to see such a once-lovely house so dreadfully abused, but I knew it could be restored with luster.

We moved in July, 1981, and every surface was either painted, polished, papered or refinished. By October of that year, having spent a goodly sum of money secured by a second mortgage (paid for by my rental income), the house was transformed into its former glory. With all the cosmetic work I undertook, we did very little structural changing, even though I would have loved to redo the kitchen and the master bathroom. But unfortunately, they had been remodeled, or should I say botched, by earlier owners, and even though they were not aesthetically pleasing to me, I could not justify re-doing them again. That was to plague me for many years.

Eventually, in 1986, I bit the bullet and did a complete overhauling of the kitchen. It was good enough to ensure the quick and timely sale of the house two years later.

This house that I sort of, but not really, liked, but not loved – I always felt it really wasn't MY house, since it was bought by Jerry and another woman – was to be the house I and the girls lived in the longest – 7 years! Funny how life turns out. It also turned out to be the biggest money-maker. Part of that was the times. The 1980's were a period of greatest inflation, especially in housing, in our lives up to that point.

Jerry paid $113,000 for it in 1978. We added about $50,000 worth of improvements to it over the years. (Including our second mortgage, for which the interest rate was 18 percent!) We sold it in 1988 for $420,000.

For the record, the house had an awkward floor plan. It was top-heavy. The living room was lovely and spacious, with a wall of knotty-pine paneling and a substantial stone fireplace. The dining room was not in proportion, being long and narrow. Jerry lopped off one end of it to make a small TV room or den for the kids.

There was no other room except the kitchen on the first floor, except for a powder room under the stairs. It did have a true center hall which led to a large open porch. The second floor had a master bedroom and bath, two additional bedrooms and hall bath, and then another bedroom and bath up over the kitchen, like a maid's room. This was where Marshall hung out. He had his own private back staircase, that led down to the kitchen.

There was a third floor with two more bedrooms and a nice attic. An unfinished basement with laundry and a two car garage completed the house. The house had quality features, like plaster walls and good six-over-six paned windows, but there was something missing about the house. It was "off" by some little bit. I was very glad when the opportunity came to sell it and move on.

10 UPLAND ROAD NORTH
BEDFORD, NEW YORK 10506

CHAPTER ELEVEN

This was supposed to be our "forever" house. Both Jerry and I fell in love with it as soon as we each saw it. We saw it separately that first time. Then, later that afternoon, we went back and saw it together. I negotiated on it that same day and we had a deal. We had been planning to move to Washington, D.C. because Jerry was going to be leaving IBM to take a position at The University of Maryland. It was 1988 and the girls had one and two years respectively remaining in high school. I wasn't thrilled about changing their schools for them – and neither were they – but the opportunity for Jerry seemed very advantageous. I was ready to leave the Cherry Street house, and I thought the opportunities in the Washington area would be beneficial for the girls. I also figured they could cope, as they always had in the past, with change, especially if, as in this case, it would have been for the better. I've never liked the New York area, except for the closeness of family and friends, and I've always had a soft spot in my heart for Washington. And besides, I rationalized, it was just a one-hour plane hop from here to there. A real easy commute.

But, to my complete surprise, after we had put the Cherry Street house on the market and had a contract out on it almost instantly, Jerry got cold feet and decided he couldn't leave Big Blue after all these years. And so, since I really wanted to leave Cherry Street (it was too big for us now that Marshall and Debi were in college and it had six bedrooms and it wasn't MY house, remember?), I set out to find us a house in the girls' same school district. We wanted to make a sideways move, financially, and it was going to be difficult. After looking at many houses, from the vantage point of my profession as a broker, I was getting discouraged.

One of the agents in our office was bringing in a new listing. We all chuckled at how overpriced it was. She was unconcerned. It had "charm." That was an unquantifiable commodity. Many of the older agents in the office remembered the house from before I had been in the business. It had been the house of Linda Rogers, the daughter of Richard Rogers, the renowned composer of so many Broadway musicals. All the women in the office agreed it was a great little house with a fabulous pool on a gorgeous piece of property. The only thing they quibbled with was the price. Betsy, the listing agent, would never get that.

I was intrigued and wanted to take a look. My friend and colleague, Mary Toy, who had negotiated for me on the Cherry Street house, advised me not to waste my time looking at this little house.

"It's too small for you and it's too much money, Susan," she cautioned me. I trusted Mary and her advice, but I decided I could spare five minutes to go over and see it. Well, that five minutes changed my life. I fell in love – with a house! – again.

It was a lot more money than we had wanted to spend. How would we overcome that obstacle? I decided that we should sell our half ownership in the ski condominium we shared with our friends, the Bloms, in Breckenridge, Colorado. It was merely a transfer from one real estate investment to another, I reasoned.

I thought the value and investment potential was greater in Westchester than in Colorado – at that time, 1988. Jerry agreed with me. Our investment in Colorado had dropped considerably over the eight years we had it.

As to the small size of the house itself, we needed an extra room. It was just barely 1800 square feet. (The Cherry Street house was 3,600 square feet). The house had a beautiful large screened porch off the living room. We thought we could glass it in rather inexpensively and make that our extra room.

And so, with stars in our eyes, we moved from Bedford Hills to Bedford Village. For us, it was like moving to another planet, even though it was in the same school district. But things worked out a little differently from the way we had envisioned.

For one thing, we didn't glass in the screened porch, even though we had an architect draw up plans to do so. Once we moved into the house, on a hot, July 4th weekend, we sat out on that lovely porch, looking out over the beautiful property and we marveled. It was so cool and peaceful, with its many hemlocks, pines, rock outcroppings and a special Chinese dogwood right in front of the porch. How could we give up this porch, we asked ourselves? Well, to make a long story short, we scrapped our plans and did something different.

We decided to make an addition onto the end of the house instead. Jerry's mother, Mae Woodall, had died after we had taken title to the house, and so we had more money. We were now able to do a little more. It turned out to be quite a bit more. Instead of glassing in a porch, we built a Great Room, expanded the kitchen, and added a wet bar and a powder room off the dining room. The addition afforded us a new spacious garage, which gave us a larger basement as well. Simultaneously, we replaced most of the systems in the house and generally enlarged the house by a third. I came to understand the four most costly words in building were: "as long as we're…" and also: "we might as well…" We ended up spending quite a bit more money than we had originally anticipated, but we also got a lot more bang for the buck. And besides, we were going to be there "forever."

We were especially fortunate to have a terrific builder, Michael Wetzel, the son of a colleague at the real estate agency where I worked, Houlihan/Lawrence, Katonah, New York — Maureen Wetzel. Michael and I were on the same wave-length at every step of building and remodeling that he did at 10 Upland Road North. I had heard stories and even seen renovation and remodeling jobs that were nightmares. Adding the addition to Upland Road North was totally pleasurable. We were fortunate that we could live undisturbed in the original part of the house while the construction of the new wing was going on. And so, working with Michael and being a part of the process was, for me, a full-time and fascinating experience. It was strictly serendipitous, with very little planned ahead, except for the size of the addition.

We agreed on a basic cost and outlined the project, which Michael estimated would take about six weeks. I knew that were I to make any changes, there would be an increase in cost, so I was as careful as I could be to stay within the original framework.

The addition was about 600 square feet. That included a Great Room, with a vaulted ceiling braced by three beams. There was an enclosed breezeway of sorts connecting the Great Room with the existing dining room. We decided to install a wet bar there. When Mother came to visit one weekend, she suggested we had enough space to add a small powder room, which would come in very handy at that end of the house. And so, we followed her advice, and ended up with a smashing powder room, complete with wain-scoted walls and a marble floor.

Once the room was completely framed out, including the installation of the windows, I panicked. The far wall, as we had planned, had three windows placed evenly. There were to be book-cases in between the windows. Then I thought the middle window was unnecessary and we could better use the space for bookcases.

"Michael! I cried. "I know we agreed to three windows on that wall, but now I don't like the middle one there. What can we do?" I was so afraid of being considered a ditz.

Michael just smiled. He picked up a large piece of sheetrock that was leaning against another wall.

"You don't want the window?" he asked rhetorically. With that, he hurled the sheetrock to the wall, covering the middle window. "See, no window!" he exclaimed. We all had a good laugh over that one.

Two years after we completed the addition, Jerry woke up one morning and announced: "I'm not getting any younger. I'm taking some of my mother's money and building a tennis court!" I was stunned, but I couldn't argue with him. It was his mother's money. We had enough for our other obligations. I wasn't happy with the idea, but I honestly couldn't stand in his way. And besides, we were going to be here forever. It would be a nice enhancement to the house. We certainly had the room and the perfect spot on our four acres. It took a year to build that court, as well as more money than we anticipated (doesn't everything?) and our assessment went up, as it had before with the new addition, and so our taxes went up, but in the end, we had a spectacular tennis court. One day I noticed my two daughters, Sunny and Serena, spontaneously playing a game of tennis up there on our new court. I envisioned all sorts of family reunions around the court, the pool, and all sorts of other pleasant fantasies. I was happy we had it. Jerry, of course, was ecstatic.

The ecstasy was short-lived. One year, to be exact. The first summer that the court was playable, but not totally completed, I was unable to take advantage of it. My mother was dying of lung cancer and I was spending every possible minute with her in Farmington, Connecticut. The next year, after the court had been completed, Jerry was hospitalized with prostate cancer. He did not play tennis that season. It was at the time, anyway, that we were finalizing the painful plans to change our lives radically.

Jerry had been inundated with offers from universities before and since the one from Maryland. Now, 5 years later, in 1992, IBM's status as the premier corporation as well as the premier corporate research facility, was in serious trouble. To put it bluntly, IBM was going down the tubes. Hard to believe, but true. Now, Jerry's demand at universities was a blessing. He was also of full retirement age, having completed over 30 years of service there. The writing was on the wall and we would be foolish not to notice or take advantage of it. My mother was dead, Dad was flexible, Sunny and Serena were well into their college careers. It was time to act upon realities rather than dreams and fantasies.

We made the decision to retire from IBM and accept an advantageous opportunity with Purdue University in West Lafayette, Indiana. It had been very painful for me to acknowledge that I would be uprooting myself again and in such a drastic manner.

When we had moved into the Upland Road house, I had hoped it would be forever because I wanted to put down my roots for good. I, and my children, not to mention Jerry and his family, had moved many times. We both envisioned the Bedford house as a family homestead, where we could gather and reunite our growing and extended family. The biggest thing I'm learning out of this is that, silly girl, nothing is forever. I'm also trying to be flexible and open-minded and positive about new adventures.

We put our beloved house on the market at the end of January and we miraculously found a buyer. It was a sweet-heart deal. We got more than we expected, given the vagaries of the market. It was a terrible time to sell in Westchester County. The economy was in recession, and IBM's troubles were but an example of the economy. In 1988, we bought at the height of the market, paying $560,000 and putting in an additional $200,000 in improvements and additions. In 1993, we sold at the bottom, and yet for $100,000 more than any broker (except me) said we would: $660,000. Even though we ended up losing $100,000 on it, it was still a good financial move for us, as we were moving to an area where the cost of living was at least half of New York, and Jerry's salary was the same as at IBM and he would be receiving his IBM pension as well.

So, for five years we were able to live in a place which we considered paradise. Not everyone has that opportunity. I've taken lots of pictures of 10 Upland Road North, and that turned out to be a very prescient move.*

Where we moved, West Lafayette, Indiana, the Heartland, was not nearly as beautiful as the Northeast, but we did manage to find a house to live in that we both loved. Again, we bought it instantly.

It was meant to be a temporary house, as I was hoping to build my dream house. But after many months of looking, we weren't able to find suitable land. Just as we were making plans to renovate and remodel this expanded Cape Cod style house at 313 Leslie Avenue, serendipitously, we found a house with almost the exact floor plan that I would have built! Before I go into that house, to which we moved in 1994, let me describe the Leslie Avenue house in a little more detail in the next chapter.

*In 2005, after three additional moves, I found myself back in the state of my birth, Connecticut, and with a new man, Charles Kochakian, who would become my third husband in 2006. During our courtship, which took place in New Haven and Branford, Connecticut, I was describing my favorite house to him: 10 Upland Road North, Bedford, New York.

Not only did I want to see it again, but I thought Charles would like to see it also. I had described it in such glowing detail and enthusiasm. As it was about a little over an hour's ride from New Haven, Charles was game to see it with me.

We drove to Bedford on a Saturday and my anticipation and excitement at seeing the house I would never forget, grew stronger. We drove up from the Merritt Parkway, through New Canaan and over to Pound Ridge and Route 172, the back way. We entered the dirt road (where horses could amble) of Pine Brook and came up upon the house from the back and side. As I turned the corner from Pine Brook to Upland Road North, I saw my old house with its windows blown out and scorched wood surrounding the openings. There were no doors, but those openings were charred as well. I was shocked beyond belief! A fire in my beautiful old house!

None of my old Bedford friends had contacted me about this tragedy. What happened? I called the Bedford Fire Department on Monday to ask what happened to the house at 10 Upland Road North. A man answered and told me that the house had been sold and the new owners had given the house to the Fire Department for fire practice until it would be torn down and replaced with a much larger house. Our beautiful Bedford home was now a "tear-down!" We had put the best of everything into that house. We made sure that it would last a very long time, even if we weren't its owners anymore. And now, it would be turned into ashes. My heart broke at the news. When I told the children, their hearts broke also. Marshall and his wife, Cecilia, had been married in that house, almost 15 years before.

A year later, Charles and I returned to see what had erupted in its place. A huge Adirondack-styled McMansion overtook the property. The long beautiful driveway leading up to our little home had been filled in, and the entire orientation of the structure was changed. The pool and the tennis court were still there, but all the charm was gone. I still get so sad just thinking about it. It has been such a loss.

313 Leslie Avenue
West Lafayette, Indiana 47906

Chapter Twelve

When Jerry was first entertaining the idea of leaving Westchester County, New York, for Purdue University in West Lafayette, Indiana, I thought to myself: "never in a million years!" But you know the old adage: "never say never." It's true. Don't do it. You just might find yourself eating your words, so to speak. I did.

I had to do more than eat my words – I had to psyche myself up for even this possibility. It wasn't easy and it took a long time, but I actually did it. In the end, I was not only ready, but looking forward to it! It's amazing how we can play with our heads and our hearts.

Before leaving Bedford, we threw a Bye, Bye Bedford Barbecue. We had a tent, and Marshall's band supplied the music. I found a little place in Stamford that catered the barbecue, and we invited all our families and our friends. The weather cooperated and we had a good time. Not even any tears.

And then, we were off. We bought this house almost on a lark. We weren't planning on buying a house on that first look-see trip to West Lafayette. We were really just trying to look at land to build. This was the summer of 1992, a year before we were ready to relocate. We weren't moving to Indiana until September of 1993, but we didn't know how long it would take to find land to build. After a few days of looking, we realized it would be very hard to build from New York.

I wanted to rent a house once we moved there and then build. But the broker who was showing us the land and the area showed us this house that had just come on the market, and we were so enchanted with it and the real estate values in the Midwest that we decided to buy it – a year in advance. Jerry promised me it would be an interim house. In the meantime, of course, he fell in love with it and really didn't want to move.

Its location near the University was perfect. A ten-minute walk. The house itself was charming. Just like the house Jerry grew up in, built by his father, in Takoma Park, Maryland. It also reminded me of South State Road, and I had fond memories of that house. Once we moved into the house, it turned out to be a charmer. I met some wonderful neighbors who became very good friends and we imme-diately felt right at home. In fact, on the very day we moved into the Leslie Avenue house, as I was directing the movers as to where to put the furniture, a woman appeared at my front door.

"Hi," said the smiling face, "I'm Lila Cohen and I live right across the street, over there," she pointed to a ranch house. "I'd like to welcome you to the neighborhood. I've made some cookies and soup and some iced coffee for you."

I have never, in all my moves, been welcomed so warmly as I had that early September day.

I thanked Lila and accepted her welcome gifts and felt a warm glow in my heart.

Within that very week, Lila called and invited Jerry and me to dinner at her house to meet more neighbors.

Lila and I had so much in common, that we could have been sisters. To our amazement, our first husbands, now dead, were attorneys; our husbands were professors in engineering at Purdue, we had both traveled extensively, due to our husbands' careers, we both had younger sisters and two children apiece, we had the same china and crystal, we both loved Black Watch Plaid... I could go on and on. We became the best of friends, and so our entry into the unknown proved smooth and enjoyable.

My family was coming to visit us for that first Thanksgiving. In The Heartland. About ten days before they were scheduled to arrive, my sister, who had been dating Guy Sherman for the past year, called me.

"Guy's asked me to marry him and we'd like to get married over Thanksgiving at your house!"

She was very happy. I said of course!

Amongst the friends I had made besides Lila were two women who lived in the neighborhood: Shirley and Linda. They were Jewish and a few years older than me. They had lived in West Lafayette for a long time. We walked together every morning from our houses into town to get The New York Times. I consulted them about the issue of my sister getting married at my house in 10 days. Who would marry them? Who would cater? Who would do the flowers? Even small weddings have lots of details and we didn't have lots of time, and besides, Thanksgiving was a busy time for everyone.

Linda, who had lived in Lafayette all her life, had all the answers. I should call Sonia Margerum, the mayor of West Lafayette, to see if she was available to perform the ceremony. I called her, and introduced myself over the phone, told her the situation, and she immediately agreed to come to our house to do the honors. I was so impressed that there was none of this "I have to check my schedule..." – everything was "yes!" And so it went with the other vendors I contacted. I concluded this new place we had chosen to live was direct, immediate, and yes. I was happy.

The wedding went off without a hitch, and it doubled as a house-warming, as we invited our new-found friends to help us celebrate the marriage of Kathe and Guy.

For the record, we paid $212,000 for this 2,700 square foot house, built in 1960. It was on a half acre, on a city street, with sidewalks, and city sewers and city water. That was something we hadn't enjoyed in years. The property taxes were $2,800 a year, as compared with the taxes on our Bedford house, which were over $13,000. As you can see, the cost of living in Indiana is far less than in New York. At the time, we also felt the quality of life was curiously better, because it was open and unpretentious. The downsides, which didn't begin to grate on us until a few years later, were a lack of beauty in the land, and a total lack of such amenities as decent restaurants, shopping and culture.

Back to 313 Leslie Avenue, after much angst and looking at land and even other re-sales to either redo or tear down and rebuild, we came to the conclusion that we'd be best served by renovating this house to our own taste. The location was perfect for us. And then one Sunday we were invited to a brunch at a new friend's house. It was about 5 miles out of town, in a lovely neighborhood. I remarked to Jerry as we drove towards it,

"Gee, it's too bad there are no more lots available to build here. This is a nice neighborhood."

We had never been there before. Our friends' house was lovely and we were impressed. The land had hills (called ravines there) and mature trees. As we were leaving the brunch to return home, we noticed a woman putting a For Sale sign in the front yard of a striking A-frame home around the corner from our friends' house. Jerry stopped the car and said,

"Wow! Look at that house! Let's find out about it — an A-frame has high ceilings. It would be perfect for my piano!"

I looked at him and the house. I was scared. Yes, the house was large and impressive. It occupied the choicest lot in the neighborhood. And yes, I did like the neighborhood. But an A-frame? I shuddered.

I called the Realtor on the sign. We learned that the house was just coming on the market and the owners were simply moving down the same street to a farm at the end of the neighborhood. They wanted more land. The house was almost 4,800 square feet on an acre of land, and it was in mint condition. The asking price was $255,000. That was all Jerry needed to hear.

"I want that house, Susan, get it for us!"

4039 Moss Creek Lane
West Lafayette, Indiana 47906

CHAPTER THIRTEEN

I'm not normally superstitious, but I note that this is Chapter Thirteen, and that the number 13 is traditionally an unlucky number. In terms of real estate, it was for us too. But who knew that in the beginning? (I did – I felt it in my bones, but I tried to ignore my instincts. I'm always trying to be positive.)

This was a house like no other either of us had ever lived in. An A-frame, it was all dark and woodsy, reminding me of a Colorado ski lodge. But Jerry wanted this house and basically promised me the sun, the moon and the stars if I were to secure it for him. He was nothing if not relentless. And so, my dreams of building a house from scratch were sublimated into acquiring this house and transforming it – whatever the cost – into something I could be proud of and enjoy.

I noted that the floor plan of this house was just what I would have built: Great Room, kitchen, and master suite on the main floor; separate family room and guest bedrooms and baths on another floor, in this case, the lower level, which was a walk-out basement. It had a three-car garage with a one-bedroom apartment over it. That would be perfect for Jerry's music studio or the girls to live in, or a graduate student, or live-in help, or whatever. The only thing I couldn't abide was the silhouette of the A-frame from the exterior. I rationalized that I wouldn't see that from the inside. And the sloping ceilings inside didn't bother me as much, because there was so much space and light. And, it was only one room that had the sloping ceilings: the Great Room, which was for Jerry's piano.

I gritted my teeth and did my very best to turn this sow's ear into a silk purse. Jerry, after an initial melt-down during the chaos of actual work, eventually came to love the place.

We were fortunate to have a terrific contractor, Denny Kuhns, a German Baptist, who was a joy to work with. Here's what we did to transform this dark ski lodge of a house into something light, bright and sophisticated. First, we removed the carpeting throughout and added hardwood flooring on the first floor. On the lower level, we added new Berber carpet. We had to replace the deck, and while we were at it, we replaced the sliding doors leading from the Great Room to the deck. We also replaced the front door, which had been solid wood, with a double-French door, to let in more light.

We completely gutted the kitchen, which had been a "country kitchen" with dusty rose and denim blue wallpaper, into a sleek, contemporary specimen with a professional grill and exhaust system, as well as all top of the line professional appliances. I designed the bleached maple cabinets and all the work was exe-cuted by another team of German Baptist workers, who again, were a joy to work with. We eliminated upper cabinets, due to my height (I'm five foot one) and the lower cabinets were all pull-out drawers. The cook-top was designed to be 4 inches lower than the counters, as my research discovered that the French like to "look down into the pot." The counters were creamy white Corian and the floors were Mexican 12 inch square tiles.

Additionally, I brought from the Leslie Avenue house a crystal chandelier from the dining room that I loved. I put it in my new sleek contemporary kitchen and it became the focal point of conversation. It added a sense of "je ne sais quoi." Another bit of whimsy was the three clocks I installed over the kitchen sink. One was for Indiana time, one was for New York (Serena) time, and one was for San Francisco (Sunny) time.

We redid the master bath to include a custom-made marble tub (I went to the showroom and lay down in a model, so the dimensions would be comfortable for my small frame), which I rarely used because I prefer showers to tub baths. It was all for re-sale, of course.

There was a loft area overlooking the Great Room, which was transformed into an office for me, with custom-built cherry cupboards and desk. And of course, the lighting proved problematic, as the entire first floor was all cedar planking, and so wiring had to be installed with tracking. But the real transformation occurred by painting all the dark cedar walls and ceiling white. I was told afterwards that it would have been cheaper and easier to simply sheet-rock them. But I did admire the texture of painted wood surfaces. It reminded me of the house on Beech Tree Lane of my childhood. As the painter later admitted to me, it was a good thing the walls were strong and solid, as the weight of so much paint would never have been supported by walls of lesser strength or material.

Part of the house had a flat roof, over the garage and the master suite area, and within two years of our residence, we had to replace it, as it began to leak after an ice storm. That set us back about $35,000. In total, we ended up spending as much in remodeling and repairs as we spent on the initial purchase price, which of course, was the asking price of $255,000. In so doing, we priced ourselves out of the neighborhood, but we didn't care, as we were going to be in this house "forever."

Once I remodeled Moss Creek, however, I was left with a void in my life. I was taking some writing courses at Purdue, which I enjoyed immensely, but it wasn't leading to anything. I tried for awhile to write a column for the local paper. I got a few columns published, but couldn't manage to turn it into a paying position. I chaired a Decorator's Show House for a benefit and that was very successful. But it had limited use, even though I was hoping to turn that endeavor into something professional. What, I didn't have a clue.

I tried getting a job in development at Purdue. Jerry did the best he could in trying to use his considerable influence to get that going, but it didn't happen. Meanwhile, Yale University was pursuing him to come to New Haven. Needless to say, that prospect appealed to me more than ever. I was getting very bored in Indiana and I missed my family. I thought Jerry would enjoy Yale and the East Coast, with all its culture and our old friends, even though most of them had moved to other places.

Jerry pointed out to me that Purdue was THE place for electrical engineering, his field, and not Yale. Nevertheless, he was intrigued by being pursued by such a prestigious institution. When things started to go sour for him at Purdue (grant money drying up) I saw this as an opportunity to push for the position at Yale. And push I did. I prayed very hard too. It finally worked.

One of the happiest days of my life was that November day in 1998 when we flew to New Haven for one last talk with the provost, Alison Richard. She had told Jerry she was going to pursue him until he said yes. On that day, Jerry finally did. It had been over two years of on-and-off negotiations between Jerry and Dick Barker, a colleague and professor of Electrical Engineering, and an alumnus of Yale as well. I was so excited, I jumped up and hugged Jerry right in Alison's office. The clincher was that she promised to use her influence to get me a job at Yale, something that hadn't happened at Purdue. Yale had just instituted a new program for people like me, a "trailing spouse." It included counseling, place-ment and some very minimal computer training.

During that very meeting, Alison picked up the phone and arranged for me to meet with several people in Yale's Central Development Office. Within ten minutes, a woman there, Martha Schall, came by to escort me around campus and to the Development Department. She took me to lunch at Mory's, the esteemed old private eating club on campus, and I was a goner.

Along with the excitement of coming to Yale, was the prospect of moving and trying – again – to build a house of my own.

But before we go into that, I want to mention another of my beloved real estate purchases: a condominium in downtown Chicago.

330 West Diversey Parkway
Chicago, Illinois, 60657

CHAPTER FOURTEEN

I bought a unit in this condominium building as part of a 1031 tax exchange, which is a device to postpone capital gains taxes on real estate. This transaction occurred when I sold the South State Road house in anticipation of moving to Indiana. I had made a huge capital gain on it, having owned it from 1978 to 1993. To avoid (postpone, really) paying the capital gain, Uncle Sam allowed investors to re-invest the money, within six months of the sale, in a like-kind exchange. What a problem for me – not!

With part of the money, I bought a small rental house in West Lafayette. It was just a place to park money. Nothing worth mentioning otherwise. But I wanted to invest in Chicago. I thought eventually, somehow, we could turn the investment property into a pied-a-terre for us.

I went up to Chicago (which was a two and a half hour drive from West Lafayette) twice and saw a couple of Realtors. I told the second Realtor I would like views of Lake Michigan and wanted to be near the Miracle Mile (Michigan Avenue.) I wanted to spend about $200,000. This was 1994. You could purchase some very nice properties there for that price.

The Realtor listened to me and took me to the first property. She admitted that it wasn't quite within walking distance of Michigan Avenue and said no more.

It was a Mies Van der Rohe building, of which there are quite a few in Chicago. I had seen other Mies buildings previously; they all have the same feel. But when we opened the door to this particular apartment, facing south, on the 24th floor, and I saw the views of not only Lake Michigan to the left, but the whole of Lincoln Park and the Chicago skyline in front of me, I gasped. The views, from all floor-to-ceilinged windows in all the rooms, were breath-taking. I looked at a few other condos afterwards, just to make sure, but I instantly bought this one, again, paying full price and loving every minute of it. It was a good deal.

The unit, 2 bedrooms and 2 baths, had been updated, except for the baths, which were "original Mies." Of course, I would be renting it out, due to the terms of the like-kind exchange, but I hoped to eventually be able to live there part-time myself.

When we left the Midwest for Connecticut I didn't want to sell the condo and so I made Sunny an offer she couldn't refuse. She could live there, pay the common charges, which were less than her current rent, and keep the place warm for us, so to speak. Part of the deal was that we could stay there if and when we visited Chicago. As it turned out, we rarely visited, and when we did, we stayed at hotels.

Sunny moved from San Francisco to West Diversey Parkway in the winter of 1998. I knew she would love Chicago: it has great culture; a thriving art scene, and the weather is cold, which she loves. She would not need a car, as she doesn't drive. Even though

I eventually had to sell the condo, Sunny still lives in Chicago and loves it. And I have great memories, of that apartment and of Chicago itself. It came to be my favorite city in the United States.

64 RIMMON ROAD
WOODBRIDGE, CONNECTICUT 06525

CHAPTER FIFTEEN

Once the details of Jerry's job as a distinguished professor of electrical engineering, with a side appointment in applied physics, were set in place, I set out to find a place to live as close to the Yale campus as possible. Jerry was not interested in commuting and I was so grateful to him for bringing me "home" to Connecticut that I wanted to make him as happy as possible.

My sister lived in Westport, which was a big reason to move back. I had been hoping my Dad would still be alive, but he passed away just a few months before we knew we were coming. He would have been so happy. Serena was ensconced in New York City and I hoped she would stay there or at least on the East Coast. Sunny was in San Francisco and not thriving. I was hoping she would move to Chicago – to our fabulous condo, and it turned out, she did.

My sister put me in touch with a Realtor in New Haven, Sheila Weinberg. One of those small world stories, Sheila had been my babysitter when I was an infant! Her parents and mine were old and good friends, Sylvia and Charlie Schechtman, from New Britain. We discovered this as we were talking on the phone, me in Indiana and Sheila in New Haven.

I told Sheila my first choice would be to build a new house. I suspected it would be more expensive than we wanted it to be. Moving back from the Midwest to the East Coast was not the same as moving in the opposite direction. We were now moving back to a more expensive place to live, although not nearly as expensive as Bedford, New York. I was also amenable to finding a re-do.

We stumbled upon a colonial house in Woodbridge, where we decided to live because of its proximity to Yale and the avoidance of commuting on I-95, that was under construction. It was a house built on speculation. The studs were up and it was ready to go. It was at the point where you could add all the finishing work and customize it. I hadn't really wanted a colonial, but it was a good compromise: affordable, ready to be finished in a reasonable time frame, and a good location. My sister saw it and said to me:

"Susan, you should consider this house. It could work for you." She was right. I showed it to Jerry and he, not wanting to get involved at all, but rather concentrating on the change in his career, let me have full reign in the real estate department. That was a blessing, I thought. Again, I wanted to keep things as smooth as I could for him.

We put a bid on the colonial, but we were a few days too late. It went to another family. We met with the builder, Joe Carotenuto, who seemed quite affable at the time. Very eager to please and, I thought, easy to work with. My past experiences with contractors had been so positive, that I just assumed it would continue. Wishful thinking, but I'm getting ahead of myself.

"So, you like the house, huh?" Joe asked me with a smile. "Tell ya what. I have another lot that's better than this one. I'll build you the same house for the same price on it. How's that?"

I looked at him. Did this sound too good to be true? It sure did to me. I said to him cautiously,

"OK Joe, show me the lot. If it really is better than this one, you've got a deal. Of course, I want to make some changes and modifications to this house. Is this OK with you?'

Joe gave me that knowing smile again. "Sure, you can make any changes you want – you'll just have to pay for them. Course, I'll give you a real good deal."

Well, we drove around the corner from this house that had just been sold out from under us and down another street, still very close by, and I saw the lot. Wonder of all wonders, it did look better to me than the first one. There was more property, bordered by wetlands, the lot was deep and nicely wooded; the neighboring houses were mixed enough so a new colonial would not upset the status quo of the neighborhood. I was puzzled. It did seem too good to be true. I told Joe I liked the lot and I would think seriously about it. He looked a little peeved.

"I'm not gonna hold it for you for long, Susan," he said intimidatingly. "You'd better make a decision quick." I had a sense of forboding then, that if I didn't play ball Joe's way, he wouldn't be as affable as he first appeared. He could be threatening. I figured I could handle him.

I did some investigating about him; checked his references, contacted some recent satisfied clients, and within a short time, we signed a contract. Our attorney, Stephan Hilcoff, obtained through my sister, was very skeptical of Joe. But we stubbornly pushed forward.

Here's what we got: the base price was $425,000. For that we got 2.67 acres of land on a main road (not a problem for me but it would figure in a resale), across the street from a conservative synagogue, B'Nai Jacob, and barely five miles from Jerry's office at Yale. A 4,000 square foot colonial house with 3-car garage, a screened porch (one of my priorities) a deck, hardwood floors, or tile of our choosing, the ability to plan the layout pretty much to our specifications, which was the biggest attraction for me, and a hook-up to town water, no well. Of course, we went to town with extras. Just as in Moss Creek and Beford before that, we chanted the mantra: "we might as well," and "as long as we're..." Jerry, true to form, wanted state-of-the-art everything: heating, cooling, plumbing, etc. I was worried about the windows. Should they be vinyl for ease-of-maintenance, or wood for quality? The ones Joe used weren't a brand I had heard of. I obsessed over those windows, even though I liked the way they looked and operated.

We ended up spending, when all was said and done, about $45,000 more than the base price of the house, but we got a cus-tom-tailored house. I was still thrilled. As it was, we both felt we were getting a good deal.

And then the fun began. We upgraded everything. Our hot water heater was large enough to satisfy an apartment complex. Jerry wanted a music room, otherwise known as the dining room, and he wanted it sound-proofed. For the first time in either of our lives, we added a sump pump and a generator – just in case.

I wanted a walk-in, or rather a roll-in shower. I had visions, nightmares of my father in a nursing home, unable to stand or walk, being hoisted on a pulley into a common shower. The indignity of that memory was seared on my brain and I vowed to have a house with universal design that would satisfy our needs as we aged or became handicapped. Hence, the walk-in-shower. No threshold, no step, no lip. No doors to fall against and crash through, as happened to my father's good friend, Victor Fassler. The dimensions of the shower were 5 feet by 8 feet and it had multiple shower heads on two walls. A wheelchair could easily roll right in. We had separate vanities, Jerry and I, as Jerry would never put down the toilet seat on principle, and so I never had to even see his commode, nor he mine. He wanted a bidet as well.

I wanted a laundry room on the second floor. There was a laundry room on the first floor which we turned into a mud/utility room. It housed the Sub-Zero refrigerator/freezer we brought from Moss Creek, and we kept the plumbing in for laundry hook-ups, just in case.

Jerry wanted a heated garage and so all 3 bays were centrally heated. The kitchen was a marvel, in my humble opinion. Building on the success of my first design at Moss Creek, I refined the design somewhat. Instead of a tile floor, which I found hard and cold, we now had a wood floor. Again, I eliminated upper cabinets, and added all pull-out drawers for the lower ones. I made sure they were shallow so I wouldn't have to reach too far in the back. We had an island, 8 feet by 3 feet, topped in granite, as were all the counters. The island became a beautiful buffet server. A professional gas range, with an even bigger hooded vent, as well as a deck with built-in gas grill made cooking a snap. I eliminated the warming drawer here (I had installed it in Moss Creek, in homage to Overton Road), as I felt it was a health hazard and I didn't use it enough anyway. The kitchen opened to the family room, with a gas fireplace and a large TV screen, viewable from the kitchen,

I eliminated a formal living room, since it would have been a waste of space. People always seemed to congregate in the kitchen-family room. We enlarged the dining room to accommo-date the Steinway and the harpsichord, as well as our large table and a few other pieces. What would have been a living room became a small study for Jerry and his keyboard and computer. My office was a large high-ceilinged room over the garage. It shared that space with a guest bedroom and bath, both over-sized.

We had all these lovely features, including a huge master bed-room, a dressing room for me and merely a walk-in closet for Jerry; large windows, and my pride and joy, a screened porch (although it didn't compare to the Bedford porch). Nevertheless, the house was not emotionally warm. It had that sterile, new-house feel to it, that I had tried so hard to avoid. But it wasn't just the newness of the construction that made the house feel cold. It was the growing estrangement between Jerry and me.

Our marriage had been very unsatisfying to me for a number of reasons. I knew going into it that it would not be ordinary. I was, after all, his third wife. The Rimmon Road house was the scene of our divorce. It was just too much: Jerry's dissatisfaction with Yale, much to my astonishment, just became another complication.

In July of 1999, Jerry carried me over the threshold of our new house; my wish for building a new house fulfilled, like a first-time bride.

In January 2002, after 20 years of marriage, he moved out and into a 2 bedroom condo in downtown New Haven, near his office. The plan was that once I found a suitable place to live, either a small house or a condo, I too would move. We would sell the house and split the proceeds. A year later, that is exactly what hap-pened. In January 2003, I found exactly the condo I was waiting for: Whitney Grove Condominiums. I moved into it in May of that year, sold Rimmon Road, and our divorce became final in June, 2003.

One of the unfortunate consequences of the divorce was that I had to sell my beloved condo in Chicago, where Sunny was living. She was totally understanding about it, even though it forced her to move into smaller quarters. She acted as my real estate agent, and sold it to her next-door neighbor, who broke through to his unit and ended up with a much bigger place. It was a very easy transaction. He paid my asking price and I avoided a commission, for the first time in my life, since Leawood Drive! And he did well too. The real estate market had started to take off, while the stock market tanked.

———◆———

40 TEMPLE COURT
NEW HAVEN, CONNECTICUT 06511

Chapter Sixteen

The thought of getting divorced was terrifying to me for many reasons. The obvious ones, like the absence of love, the admittance of failure, the lack of security, both emotional and financial, of course. But, the loss of place where I would live, the concrete image of a dwelling, was the one aspect that petrified me more than anything else. For, as you have seen throughout this book, my sense of identity was totally integrated with where I lived. It still is.

I knew I wanted to live in downtown New Haven, after exploring other options like Fairfield, where I worked (miserably), and the suburbs, both for small houses and condos. I decided that since I was a single, I would be a cosmopolitan one, as best I could. I hadn't lived in an urban dwelling full-time since my college days, and I always thought of myself as a country mouse, not a city mouse. But, this was a new situation for me, and I was trying to carve out a new identity: sophisticated urban woman. Living in downtown New Haven, which was undergoing a renaissance at the time, was my goal.

New Haven is a curious city of 125,000. It is a city of literally black and white. Very cosmopolitan, with the Yale component, like a miniature version of New York or Boston. And yet, because of its size, very manageable. But there is another side to New Haven: it has one of the largest welfare populations in the state, if not, proportionately in the country. Politically, extremely liberal, it attracts a large poor and minority population due to the many social service agencies there.

The driving social, cultural, and intellectual force is Yale University. And that is a very large force. Yale is world-class and New Haven is the beneficiary of it. I wanted to be part of that. Now that I was divorced from a distinguished Yale professor, I would have to do it on my own. I started by determining to live in the best place in town I could afford. And that was unquestionably Whitney Grove Condominiums. Ironically, Jerry had wanted to live there when we first came to town, but I was adamant about building a house, as he had promised I could. Whitney Grove was directly behind Jerry's office at Yale. It was on Yale-owned land, designed by the renowned architect, Herbert S. Newman & Partners. Coincidentally, the developer, Lawrence of Bronxville, New York, was part of the establishment of Houlihan/Lawrence, where I had worked as a real estate agent back in the 1980's.

Whitney Grove is in the heart of downtown New Haven and adjacent to the Yale campus. It is a series of red brick townhouses, some on a main street and most on a private cul-de-sac, off the main street. It reminds me of Louisburg Square in Boston, or something you might see in London. Utterly charming, sophisticated and impressive. Just what I wanted. Little did I know at the time that most of the residents were Yale professors or high staff people. That made it even better. The units practically never came on the market; they went by word of mouth, and at high premiums.

I let it be known that I wanted to purchase a unit. Dogs were allowed. One day, I got a call from a Realtor I barely knew, that a unit was available. To make a short story even shorter, I made a mental note that unless there was something drastically wrong with the unit, I would buy it. I had never been inside the units; I just knew I wanted to live there. True to form, once I walked inside, I knew it was perfect for me. I made an offer over the asking price and avoided any contingencies. A deal made in heaven for the seller. He took it. I was ecstatic and it made my divorce almost seem justified. At least, it verified the old maxim: "Living well is the best revenge." I was determined.

Jerry and I split our assets equally. I spent proportionately more of my assets on this piece of real estate than I probably should have. I certainly didn't need as much space as this townhouse had, but, as I said before, I was making a statement. I rationalized it as "investing" my money. I figured I was buying a blue chip stock that would never lose its value. Plus, I would enjoy living in it while it appreciated. The dividend.

The townhouse was 3 stories: 2 bedrooms and 2,350 square feet. Built in 1988, it was quality construction, with well-appointed kitchen and baths. Nine foot ceilings on the first floor, and a lovely Trex deck terrace overlooking Woolsey Hall, the Yale campus and the New Haven skyline. It was directly behind Saint Mary's Church, which has the highest steeple in the City. The price included a spot for one car in an underground garage, which was accessed by walking outside a few steps.

The rooms were spacious, the stairway comfortable, the light was good. A fireplace in the living room, with a lovely bay window overlooking the front. Interesting neighbors and walking distance to all the cultural and social amenities New Haven has to offer. I was in heaven!

I made some minor improvements. It didn't need painting or carpeting: both were in excellent condition. I added 2 closets to alcoves separating the living room from the dining room, as well as some recessed lighting, a gas log for the fireplace, and some window treatments. And then I moved in. I did all my own packing from Rimmon Road and all my own unpacking. I took a week off from work to do it, and when Sunday evening came, all cartons had been unpacked and removed, all pictures and art were on the walls, all things were put away in their closets or drawers. I felt very fortunate that Jerry and I had as amicable divorce as we did. We had no issues as to who would get what, in terms of furniture or things. Both of us had brought certain items into the marriage from our previous lives, and those we each kept. As for the things we acquired during our 20 year marriage, it was more a question of what would fit in Jerry's new apartment, first, as he was the first to move, and then, what each of us wanted. I have to say I don't think either of us was greedy, in any way.

When it came time to sell Rimmon Road, I did give away lots of stuff, both to charity and to Marshall and Cecilia, as there would be no room at Temple Court for an entire household's worth of furniture. But, whatever I did keep fit in very nicely in the new and spacious condo. I didn't have to purchase any new pieces.

I did have a little consternation in placing my sofa and television in the new living room. I wanted the sofa to face the large bay window, and be adjacent to the fireplace. But the television cable outlet was in the wrong place! Enter my daughter, Serena, who came up from New York City, where she was living at the time, to figure out a solution to my dilemma.

We simply had the outlet rewired to another part of the wall, so that the television could be placed where I wanted it. It was then that I realized Serena was a chip off the old block, and following in the tradition of my mother, her grandmother, and me, had within her gene pool, the decorator gene. It always helps to have a fresh pair of eyes, especially of a different generation and perspective.

I didn't move anything again until I moved — again! 3 years later, from a place I thought I'd be carried out head first. But that was not to be. As in the past, my forever place was slightly less than that. But this time, for a good reason.

375 RACE HILL ROAD
MADISON, CONNECTICUT 06443

CHAPTER SEVENTEEN

I had already fallen in love with the man who would become my third husband. He had a quiet and subtle way of surprising me with delight.

We had been haphazardly looking at houses in contemplation of sealing our relationship in marriage, when he drove me and his ten-year old daughter up a winding country road, far away from where we had been looking at real estate previously.

I fell in love with the road as soon as we turned onto it. There were lots of mature trees, and a little pond right at the beginning of the road. A small white cottage and then a wood-roofed and cedar-shaked ranch, and then a barn red antique house behind a stone wall hugging the right side of the road, and then a curve and then a few more antique homes, dating back to the early eighteenth century, all now quietly updated and habited.

As we ascended the gently sloping hill, it gradually got steeper and I saw something on the right and the left that I had always loved: paddocks and open fields! There were horses on this road. It brought me back to my favorite place: Sunny Field Farm in Bedford, New York, near where I had lived in another life.

"Charles," I gasped. "This is beautiful!"

He had the real estate classifieds in between us in the front seat, with a small circle around one of the ads.

"I've always loved this road," he said softly. "Nathaniel had a friend who lived up here."

As the hill crested and leveled off, I saw two new homes, far more impressive in their mass and landscaping than the previous antiques, but just shy of being "McMansions." They were tasteful and blended in with the land appropriately.

We kept going and looking to the left were vistas of breath-taking beauty. We were high up on the hill. Another large horse farm with a dressage ring to the right and then, on the left, a small Realtor's sign pointing down a long narrow driveway.

It was January but there was no snow; it was just cold and bleak, but sunny. We stopped the car at the garage with its mock barn doors. A front porch with large white pillars beckoned us. It was a Federal-style farmhouse, brand new.

"Charles," I remarked. "This is gorgeous, but it's so expensive. How can we afford this? Why are you teasing me with something we can't have?"

We hadn't even gone in the front door yet and I was already in love with the setting and the exterior of this house.

When I looked at the ad in the paper, the price was over $100,000 more than we had agreed upon spending.

"Don't worry," my fiscally ultra-conservative lover replied with a smile, "we can afford this."

The Realtor was having an open house and we opened the front door to a welcome "hello" from somewhere unseen.

Walking down the wide hallway, noticing a small room off to the left, and stairs going up the two- story entrance to the right, we turned a corner to search for the friendly voice.

There was the Realtor, host, in the kitchen. She cordially invited us to walk around, and just inhale the views and the floor-plan. The beautifully-appointed kitchen gave way to a breath-taking large room with views and a deck overlooking the magnificent vistas we had seen on the approach to the property. The room beyond the kitchen, a family room, perhaps, was faced on three sides with large windows and French doors to the deck. A brick fireplace with elegant molding on the mantle was in front of us.

All three of us, me, Charles, and his daughter, Anna, were in love.

"Daddy, buy this house, please!" pleaded Anna.

Charles was already going up the stairs to the second floor, while Anna and I were inspecting the first floor.

Speaking of floors, in this house they were memorable and something I had never seen before, even in all my years in real estate, which ended almost 15 years earlier. The floors at 375 Race Hill were wide-planked Southern yellow pine with a smooth semi-gloss finish. They looked almost like moiré silk, as my sister would remark when she first saw them. They extended throughout the house on both floors.

The kitchen was also memorable. The cabinets were wood, painted antique yellow, in a traditional style, the backsplashes were tumbled marble tile, and the counters were granite — the very same granite that Jerry had chosen for our house in Woodbridge, at 64 Rimmon Road. I felt at home already.

The kitchen extended to a breakfast area, bounded at the end by a double window, which overlooked the back yard and the lovely views. This entire area opened to the family room, with its windows and French doors leading to a deck and the stupendous views. A brick fireplace with a finely-finished mantel and hearth was centered on the far long wall. The whole effect was open and light.

Completing the first floor was a formal dining room with glass doors, wainscoting, and wall sconces, a powder room with a pedestal sink (which I disliked) and commode, and the first room we had passed upon entering, a small formal living room. I immediately decided that this room would be the library or my office or a combination thereof, should we be so fortunate as to be able to own this house.

We climbed the stairway in the front hall and turned to the right. It was the master suite. Upon first entering it, there was a lovely spacious bathroom, with the same tumbled marble tile that was in the kitchen and was coincidentally the same tile Jerry and I had chosen for our bathrooms in the Woodbridge house. This bathroom had a double vanity, a spacious stall shower and a huge whirlpool tub. The commode was separated from all by an enclosure. There was also a linen closet in the bathroom, and a double window overlooking the back yard.

Next in the suite were two large walk-in closets, facing each other in a short hall, which led to a huge bedroom. It was the size of the oversized two-car garage underneath. The bedroom had two large windows on two walls, and a sloping ceiling at one end of it. I can now report that in addition to the queen bed and chests on either side of it, the room contains a dresser, a dressing table, a side chair, a chaise lounge, a desk and chair, a coffee table, a large leather sofa, a bookcase and a TV on a stand. And it still doesn't look or feel cluttered!

Coming back out into the hall, there was a laundry room, with a white-tiled floor — just like the one we had in Woodbridge! — another spacious bedroom facing the front of the house, with a large walk-in closet — which Anna immediately claimed for herself, a spacious hall bath, another smaller bedroom, and at the end of the hall, another bedroom with sloping ceilings and 2 dormered closets. Even though this room was over the family room, we immediately dubbed it "the room over the garage," in reference to the house Charles had in Branford, which was used as his children's play/game room. This room would serve the same function here. We now call it "the Moose Room" in homage to our annual visits to Rangeley, Maine, where moose are more than a metaphor.

After viewing the bedroom floor, we raced down to the basement, which was so large and open that we could imagine Charles' ping pong table taking up only one small area of it.

The house had central vacuum, special speakers in the ceilings of the first floor for stereo, and other amenities that bespoke a house of quality.

Charles, Anna and I exited the house and found ourselves in a dream-like state. We had seen our dream house and it would work for us. The issue of the price was overcome by Charles. He reasoned that with both of us selling our present places, we would be able to buy this house and I would have money left over, as my condo was worth more than his house in Branford.

There was very little we would have to do to the house, as it was almost completed, except for certain light fixtures, and landscaping.

The road to acquiring 375 Race Hill was convoluted and bumpy. It took two separate negotiations on two separate occasions to actually get it, but that's another story. In the end, we purchased the house in June, 2006. I moved in July of that summer and Charles moved in August. In October of that year we were married.

As of this writing, nearly six years later, I am still in love with the house and I think Charles is too. And, we're still in love with each other, so that's the real good news.

We've landscaped it, including some lovely stone walls and steps leading from one level of the yard to another; added some built-in bookcases in my office and in the family room. We've papered the walls of the powder room and our bathroom. We've painted most of the rooms, but not all. And we're now embarking on some maintenance and repair work.

Both our possessions and furniture from our previous homes fit together nicely here, and the only new piece of furniture we've bought is our bed.

Charles did have to buy a new car after two years, as his Volvo could not make it up the driveway in snow, even after it had been plowed. He now has an Audi. My all wheel-drive BMW never gave me any trouble with our driveway.

Due to the hurricane in the summer of 2011 and the snow-storm of October of that year, we lost our electric power for many days. We then decided to install a whole-house generator in 2012.

We both hope we can remain in this house for a very long time. I can even imagine retrofitting it with an elevator or first-floor bed and bath, should we require it in our old age. I hope it won't be necessary.

Financial details: in June, 2006, we paid $685,000. The house has 3,300 square feet and almost 4 acres of land. We've added another $60,000 to it over the five years of ownership to date. We have no mortgage on it. Taxes are around $10,000.

One life, 67 years of age, 17 different addresses, three husbands, two daughters, two step-sons, two step-daughters, one grandchild, and another on the way. It all adds up to quite a life, I think.

Index to Names Appearing in
My Address Book: A Way of Remembering

Alison Richard, Provost of Yale University, 1998

Anna Kochakian, daughter of Charles Kochakian

Betsy Forrester, real estate agent at Houlihan/Lawrence, Katonah, New York, 1988

Bill Bishop builder of Beech Tree Lane house

Carolyn Dwyer, Owner/Broker, Carolyn Dwyer Real Estate, Briarcliff Manor, New York

Cecilia Woodall, wife of Marshall Woodall

Chandler Woodall, 1st son of Jerry Woodall

Charles Kochakian, husband of Susan Woodall

Debi Woodall Draper, daughter of Jerry Woodall

Denny Kuhns, builder/contractor, West Lafayette, Indiana

Dick Barker, a/k/a Richard Barker, Professor Emeritus, Yale University, Department of Electrical Engineering

Emil Brandt, friend of Max and Therese Kirshnit

Emory Corbin, previous owner of 9 Laurel Road, New Britain, Connecticut

Gerard and Bela Blom, friends of Jerry Woodall and co-owners of Breckenridge, Colorado condo

Grandma and Grandpa: Sadie and Lou Blumenkopf, parents of Therese Kirshnit, Susan Woodall's mother

Guy Sherman, husband of Kathe Sherman

Harold and Suzanne Mellin: long-time friends of Steve and Susan Golding, now Woodall

Irwin Rozinsky, previous owner of 6 Leawood Drive, Briarcliff Manor, New York

Jerry Woodall, second husband of Susan Woodall

Joe Carotenuto, builder of 64 Rimmon Road, Woodbridge, Connecticut

Kathe Sherman, sister of Susan Woodall

Katie and Stan Duncan, neighbors to 9 Laurel Road, New Britain, Connecticut (children Teddy and Tootie, a/k/a Grace)

Lila Cohen, friend from West Lafayette, Indiana

Linda Cohen, (no relation to above) friend from West Lafayette, Indiana

Linda Rogers Emory, former owner, 10 Upland Road North, Bedford, New York

Mae Woodall, mother of Jerry Woodall

Marshall Woodall, 2nd son of Jerry Woodall

Martha Schall, Development Office, Yale University, 1998

Mary Toy, friend and colleague, Houlihan/Lawrence, Katonah, New York

Maureen Wetzel, friend and colleague, Houlihan/Lawrence, Katonah, New York and mother of Michael Wetzel

Michael Wetzel, builder, 10 Upland Road North, Bedford, New York

Molly and Buddy Raphael, neighbors of Therese and Max Kirshnit

Mother and Father: Therese and Max A. Kirshnit

Nathaniel Kochakian, 2nd son of Charles Kochakian

Nick Kochakian, 1st son of Charles Kochakian

Serena Jane Golding Woodall Berra, 2nd daughter of Susan and Stephen Golding, adopted by Jerry Woodall

Sheila Weinberg, Realtor for 64 Rimmon Road, Woodbridge, Connecticut and daughter of Sylvia and Charles Schechtman, friends of Max and Therese Kirshnit

Shirley Janick, friend from West Lafayette, Indiana

Sonia Margerum, Mayor of West Lafayette, Indiana, 1993

Sunny Leigh Golding Woodall Fawkes, 1st daughter of Susan and Stephen Golding, adopted by Jerry Woodall

Susan, Keefe, and Jessy Werner, friends and neighbors, Briarcliff Manor, New York

Stephan Hilcoff, attorney

Steve, Stephen L. Golding, late husband of Susan Woodall and father of Sunny and Serena

Stu Hauser, classmate of Steve Golding from Brown University.

Victor Fassler, friend of Max Kirshnit

Made in the USA
Charleston, SC
09 July 2012